Break

also by Adam Levon Brown

Musings of a Madman
These Streets Don't Cry for Us
Death Is Not Our Holy Word
Love Letters to a Ghost Named C
Loco Motion of Life
Living on The Fringe: Poetry for the Outsider
Embedded Memories of a Shooting Star
Angelic Hymns of a Life Once Burdened
Klonopin Meets Sisyphus
Anima (forthcoming)

Break

Poems on Mental Illness
by
Adam Levon Brown

Poetic Justice Books & Arts
Port Saint Lucie, Florida

©2019 Adam Levon Brown

book design and layout: SpiNDec, Port Saint Lucie, FL
cover image: *Beneath a Dream*, 2018, Kris Haggblom

All rights reserved.

No part of this book may be used or reproduced in any manner whatsoever without written permission except in the case of brief quotations embodied in critical articles and reviews. Members of educational institutions and organizations wishing to photocopy any of the work for classroom use, or authors, artists and publishers who would like to obtain permission for any material in the work, should contact the publisher.

Printed in the United States of America.

Published by Poetic Justice Books
Port Saint Lucie, Florida
www.poeticjusticebooks.com

ISBN: 978-1-950433-03-2

10 9 8 7 6 5 4 3 2

Adam Levon Brown's remarkable collection, Break, shaped as a connected series of poems of address, takes us with shaking hand and clear voice through the heart of family trauma, into the life that must cope with its consequences, and salvage from the nearly final wreckage the means not only of survival, but transcendence. It is a gift of light derived through confrontation, narrative inquiry, persistent yearning to say what is needed, and an arrival at voice that eclipses the narrative project. The poem-by-poem evolution of language matching, with near perfection, voice to journey elevates this collection from remembrance to gift.
- Marc Zegans, poet, author of La Commedia Sotterranea

Adam Levon Brown's Break is a rarity... an incredibly moving gift of poetry.
- Fee Thomas, poet, activist, author of Owning the Color Blue

Powerful and moving...Constructed in a vivid, free style verse, Brown's poems bleed anguish and heartbreak and his feelings of desperation and powerlessness show the reality of mental illness.
- The Prairies Book Review

Dear Reader,

I wrote this book with you in mind.

If you like the book (or even if you don't): Please leave a small review for it on Amazon, Goodreads, Barnes & Noble, Facebook, or wherever you purchased the book from. Without reviews from readers, books would mean nothing.

Thank you for your time.

- Adam Levon Brown

If you're interested in chatting, I'm always available online. My website and Facebook can be found below:

AdamLevonBrown.com

Facebook.com/AdamLevonBrown1

Contents

Section 1: SALTWATER
Introduction 5
Saltwater – To My Family 6
To My Pain 8
To My Trauma 9
To My First Girlfriend 13
To My Recovery 14
To My Healing 15
To Mother 16
To Father 18
Whisper – To My Brother 20
A Prayer in the Silence of Isolation – To Spirit 23
To My Heart 25

Section 2: STIGMA
Break 29
Self-Medicate –1 31
First Time in a Psychiatric Unit 32
Self-Medicate – 2 35
Pennies 36
Self-Medicate – 3 38
Branches of the Same Tree 39
Self-Medicate – 4 41
The Trauma of Spiritual Flesh 42
~~Self-Medicate – 5~~ 46
In This Society 47
To the Reader 49

Break

(Section 1)

SALTWATER

Introduction

Between the late-night movie binges, the talks, the games, and the love, my early childhood was very good

We watched football, ate tons of pizza and fast food, and had blast. My parents would give their lives for me, and they love me very much,

What I write in this book is pure honesty I do not want to criticize anyone I just want to tell my story, and heal the pain that has become too much for me to bear

As I turned 14 and entered high school, my parents went through a separation and my mother moved 60 miles away to a shelter for those with mental illness

At around this time, I found my first girlfriend, and there was a rollercoaster of both positive and negative emotions; from love, to lust, to heartbreak.

Enjoy the ride as I cascade into memories that I deem as dreams with wisps of smoke rings; shared:

Between M(ania)other and son;
between voices and father.

Saltwater – To My Family

Saltwater has a way
of cleansing small wounds
that amass during
bouts of depression

A dulled deluge of trepidation,
tasting of copper, creeping
into silent necrosis

A mouthful of sprained pain,
coughed up and abandoned
into sand dune voids

Saltwater has a way of diluting
(deluding?) the memories
staining the dull black facade,
sinister, and unspoken

A liquid slap to the stomach,
sprung from the abyss
to eat your envy and feed
off your dreams

The worst saltwater
comes from those who say
they love you, because the pure water

you're expecting, always
turns to whips of sand, laceration
becomes your heart;

seized in self-questioning,
drowning inside itself

until you barely remember
what it's like to swim

To My Pain

If I were to paint myself
the hues would speak of pain

Doused in red and black,
crimson ire soaking

the bed sheets of the mind
with sorrowful cries

Blended with narcissistic cacophony
in ears too shadow-filled to hear

Lies and guilt overshadow
the face, with lines too deep to care

The canvas is tarred and mold-ridden
from nicotine stains and a tired heart

The hands burnt red from catching moods,
chapped, nail-bitten; naked, stripped of pride

The eyes stare piteously into the abyss,
which never cares to stare back

The mouth, a lost child unhinging
lips open, hoping to speak

The hair, tangled with four
regretted seasons, braided into the sky

To My Trauma

5 years of mountains
                      strip-mined
        from
              childhood

sizzling with ugly   stares

Beaten   by bullies;
strangled   and
humiliated by my father.

Waking up to screaming,
going to school to be punched;

Coming home to alcoholism
and verbal abuse.

Watching re-runs
                of the Brady Bunch
while my mother sold food
                stamps for Vicodin.

My hope, the remains of mirrored chaos, embedded
  into a first
                girlfriend who shattered

everything that I kept hidden
                within defense mechanisms.

*

Deep cuts and cigarette burns
kept me plunging
                                      deeper into my depression;
                as the mental illness

and substance abuse
                        among all four of us grew
    deeper as well.

Constant screaming
                            from my father,
consistent hospitalizations
                            for my mother,
constant lies and betrayal
                            from those I considered friends.

Deeper my melancholy   became,   finding
    solace
only in isolation and video games.

                Dreading school every day
                      while my father screamed at me to go.

After 2 years, I had to leave –
I was already skipping classes to be "Brave"
and began hanging around drug dealers.

I was expelled for truancy. I hid
                and hid in my room.

Several days
        of my mother
            pounding
              at
                my barricaded door;

        only to escape
            when she was again
                    hospitalized for her mania
and outbursts.

My father, wouldn't look at me and grounded me
for getting expelled.

I walk with
scare stock
invested
into pockets
of paranoia

tying umbrage
to a quaking
dawn, severed
from coil.

Cast out by my
            father at 22 after having my first manic episode.

blamed by my
            reflection
for not trying harder

Now diagnosed
        with
              Schizoaffective
            disorder
                of my own,

I can at least try to
            empathize

      but I simply cannot
                condone
                      most of their
                            (lack of)
actions

                          or behavior.

To My First Girlfriend

Losing you is something
I've regretted since primitive times.

Neanderthal instincts of greed
and pride burned

the love you held for me
in a Salem-style pyre.

Bouts of alcohol-induced
anger blinded me while

scattering the ashes of
our love to the wild winds of indifference.

I slipped and fell
heart-first out of your life.

My descent quickened while I notched a mark
inside the skeleton clock of your chest.

I landed on my sorrow;
Emotional scar

That no longer bleeds,
but screams your name

every time I touch it.

To My Recovery

My language is the birth
of color, tinged with sorrow,
basking in Sun-stormed guilt

Ashen promises crumble
between icicle fingers,
grasping at an ethereal faith

When family comes
to rescue you, be wary
of your trust falling
with shattered mementos

As I peer into the mirror,
a dual reflection sees dusk
beneath the quicksilver of my eyes

I resemble fate,
as it shows nothing
but mourning
and fear

When family
becomes the scorn
inside your throat,
do you focus
on the good times?

The dynamo of my life
has cracked under my weight

My personas shiver
as I weep with mortality
on the stairways to recovery

To My Healing

The name of determination
    has embedded
    itself into my furious
    capillaries.

I bury storms
    into my back,
    collapsing hunger
    into pebbles;
    surviving on silk,
    while granite in approach.

I shy cats-eyes
    away from the hourglass
    of my dusk-burned pride.

My fury feeds on hushed
    stings, separating
    myopia from the self
    with Sun-baked hands.

Choirs of creation
    croon emerald melodies
    from my Coriander eyes,
    crying for the color Crimson,
    which cradles my trauma no longer

To Mother

I see you within St. Francis' ghost,
your frail legs carrying
the weight of men

I lean into your gentle arms,
to hug you, whispering
about the day Dad left us

I notice your shoulders
have disintegrated
mountains with their waters
of soothing voice

It's true
that I never left
you on the City bus
that coffee sky morning,
but you refuse to believe me

Dementia
has splintered
us apart

I know you spent
a lifetime harboring
the abuse and love
for two families

I know your sanity
is a prickled plumb
eating you from within

I was humiliated
at the times

you spent wavering
your voice in front
of strangers during manic episodes,
with me in tote

Now I sit by
your nursing home
bed, praying to
every God I know,

that you'll continue
to remember my face
for just one more day

To Father

I once said to you, "I'm kind of a Daddy's boy"
    You replied, "It's better than being a Momma's boy"

All the days you spent sitting in your yellow leather chair,
    omnipresent as the barn owl, watching over our tiny
    apartment, while chain-smoking and having
conversations with yourself.

I would play and play, while you stood guard;
man of the house, laying body on the line for family.

I didn't understand schizophrenia in my youth,
        and held some judgments which I now know
don't make much sense.

        You were my guardian, the protector
and my rock in this life.

        I looked up to you in ways
only children can. I saw you as Superman, as a hero,
    and as a very dutiful person who loved with every fiber
    of his being

        Now, looking back, 20 years later,
I see that you are only human, fallible, with graying hair
    just like my own.

Now that your illness has progressed beyond reassurance,

    I feel like I am standing on a pebble, reaching for
    Jupiter

You now believe you don't have to take medication
    anymore.

You have decided to be homeless 200 miles away from where my arms can reach to hug you.

                      You have muted your voice of reason, with which I relied upon for most of my life

I do not blame you.
I do not blame me.

      Blame is an easy problem, not a hard solution.

I am planning on coming to see you when the weather breaks, and when my stones of stubbornness no longer sink
my hope into vivid rivers of avoidance

                I just hope you will be there
when I arrive, though I know I will no longer
see the Superman of my childhood,

but an aged person, just looking for answers to meet daily challenges, just like myself.

      But I will I be there, just as you were there for me throughout my childhood.

If but only for a day,

to show that I haven't given up on you

      Just as you've never given up on me
To tell you, that I love you, and that I care.

Whisper – To My Brother

Something jumped into my ear
It was you, talking me down
from the roof of my mouth
which only wept one word,

"Suicide"

Something collided into my ear,
It was you, crashing the automobile
of my bumper-spinning mind
which consumed itself
in only one word,

"Death"

Something cried in my ear,
it was you, the baby carriage
I once inhabited was gone,

and I am still here, though
it sits under the mobile spinning
one word around in my eyes,

"End"

Something played music into my ear,
It was you, holding the record player
of my eardrum close to your heart,
while I considered only one word,

"Escape"

Something rattled in my ear,
it was you, holding the bottle

of pills I had planned to swallow
while ruminating on only one word,
"Deceased"

Something whispered into my ear,
It was you, reminding me of all the best
times we had together, all of the lunches,

how you taught me how to tie my shoes,
how you taught me to ride a bike, how
you always reminded me to put on my coat

before going outside, worrying
about me being cold, reminding me

of the days spent collapsing fears
with your words of guidance and your
ear of wisdom.

Your whisper changed that one
word, it changed it into danger signs

assembled en masse across every street
corner of my mind,
while reciting one word,

"Brother"

Your whisper changed that one word, it changed it into
looking at skyscrapers from the ground up, turning

them into monuments of freedom,
while reciting one word,

"Brother"
Your whisper changed that one

word, it changed it into a yearning
to have a child of my own, and a hope

that this baby will never have to face
the mobile which once haunted me,
while reciting one word,

"Brother"

Your whisper changed that one
word, it changed it into a symphony

played between us in open light,
while we laughed and no tears there to hold us down,
while reciting one word,

"Brother"

Your whisper changed that one word,
it changed into a pharmacy,
where medication

is the savior and not the enemy
to loathe and distrust,
while reciting one word,

"Brother"

Your whisper.....
Your whisper changed it all.

A Prayer in the Silence of Isolation – To Spirit

Harbinger of silent dawn;
martyr of beasts and
broken galaxies

Bring me Boethius
in handmade stars,
swept among
the dirt of past lives

Bring me the Titans
encapsulated
within supernova truth

Bring me Alexandria
cradled in the silk of mortality

Bring me destiny
wrapped in double
helix tapestry

Do not bring me saints,
for my eyes bleed
like Chrysanthemums
who sit staring at lightning

Do not bring me your broken halo,
for I have my own, resting
upon the gates of an inescapable dream

Do not bring me carnality,
for bodies are vessels
hiding behind the Maya
in circles of Niagara emptiness
Face the trembling

of the neurotic memories
of quaking dreams gripped in solar neglect

Face the trembling
of memories encircling
psychotic breaks
which once held you in static choirs

Face the trembling
of the memories,
assembling themselves into dreams,

while they scrape their iron nails
of nightmarish banshee upon the walls
of your once hallowed solace

Let us sit
within time,
grasping
for cosmos
with fingers
of clay

Let us sit inside
the Trinity, praying
for cracked Thunder

Let us stay,
Let us stay
for one more
fractured raindrop,
tasted for the finite
and swallowed

for creation's
final whimper

To My Heart

Love has been a troubadour,
    Singing
Behind curtains of reinforced steel

Broken-shuttered, starved and bare
    Jutting
From the rafters like a mad phantom

Morphing, as shapeless as shifting seabed
    Pouncing
Teeth-deep into sheet-muffled Eros

Love left deafening marks scratched,
    Naked
banished for leopard hands on icy fangs

Inhabiting Cauliflower dreams
    Ripped
From stomach, from mouth, from loins

Stones stacked in moon-drunk stumbles
    Thrown
Dancing and sacred in the name of light

        (Love)
        (Family)
        (Peace)

These words I hold as beatific
These words I cradle with withering arms
These words will never be replaced

(Section 2)

STIGMA

Break

I broke bones trying to break down the wall between me and society's expectations of me today

I began equipped with the sledgehammer of my coping mechanisms and hacked away until there was nothing left

Don't fidget when other people are looking.

I break a piece off of the wall, a piece of my security goes with it

Fidgeting is a common symptom of anxiety, this I cannot change about myself

Don't appear too weird or unusual.

I break a piece off the wall, a piece of my perception goes with it

Sometimes I appear sad or hopeless, and I have trouble controlling my facial expressions.

Don't bite your nails in public

This is a coping mechanism I learned while working with therapists to overcome anxiety

I break a piece off the wall, a piece of my perception goes with it

Don't mix up words when you talk.

I mumble a lot, and sometimes mix up my words mid-
    sentence. This is a symptom of schizoaffective disorder

I break a piece off of the wall, a piece of my personality
    goes with it

Don't think about the never-ending stigma which seems to seep into you whenever you're nervous

Stigma is the number one cause behind people experiencing mental health crises from reaching out. 1 in 4 men have or will experience mental health issues in their life.

I break down the remainder of the wall,
and the rest of myself falls with it

Self-Medicate -1

We are young,
but the only
thing on fire
is our expectation
of today

We sit and we pray
that the television
commercials
live up to their promises

As we squeeze
the last bit of lemon
into our drinks,

hoping it dulls
the bitterness
of our hearts

First Time in a Psychiatric Unit

The line sits at the pseudo-God's feet, as he sits behind a reinforced window, ready to hand out medications

    My insides begin breaking rapture with a primal scream only I can hear

        Fear is the casket which lies within

I sit idly, scratching the barcode strapped around my wrist

Breakfast, Lunch, Dinner,

the only 3 things to look forward to
when you're on hold in a psychiatric unit

Back to the line,

We stand as orderly as twin towers, waiting to swallow our next round of medication

    I learned that the blue pills
give you the best high,
    whereas the white pills make you itch

Medication is different for everyone, and I was learning the best
mix for me

    Fear is the casket which lies within

The alphabet on the calendar sitting on the wall seems to scream
at me, yelling, "Get out of here when you can."

I look away from it, and continue pacing around the 30x30 common room

    Another inpatient is rattling his head off about the government being after him.
He literally yells all day long, for hours about the same thing.

        In any other setting, he'd be terrifying, he'd be looked at as something less

In here, he was safe, in here, he had a name.

Fear is the casket which lies within

To the line again,

One of the patients I hadn't caught the name of suddenly punches the wall
and demands that he talk to his lawyer. He then runs to his 10x10 room, equipped with metal door
and begins flipping over his mattress.

        If there was a Jesus on this tiny secluded island of sterile floors and reinforced steel,
it would be him

    He then continues to berate the orderlies while kicking the wall next to my room

The orderlies act fast, and scream to one another,

"Grab the injectable, we need him settled down"

Lockdown means how it sounds.
          It means you cannot leave
What they don't tell you is that you can't really stay either

It takes a certain amount of dissociation to be able
to live under the tight, freezing cold conditions

      Fear is the casket which lies within

      I guess that's why those who don't know,
and those who think they know, but don't really know

Look at us as C|r|a|z|y

Not because we're weak, or dangerous (Though some of us
      are)

But because they can see us deal with what they consider
      insurmountable odds

and rise from our inner caskets, like a sort of Lazarus who eats
and waits in line just to pass the time

Self-Medicate - 2

Are the ghosts we try to swallow
reanimations of our fanged past?

Or are they fear of an even more vampiric future?

The nights/without/a stranger/no smell/ no stinging
sweetness/of breaths succumbed/
Calliope dancing/ with my heart

The nights/with/a stranger/scattered headaches
the/room/ like December, no Sun/to grasp

Two strangers/used as each other's dusk/
Hinged together like/broken starlight/and just as empty

Pennies

Voices lash
my brain with straps
of copper stamped zinc

Heaving themselves
upon the senses,
causing confusion,
like Cherry blossoms

which never bloomed,
but grew fangs
and tore the remnants

of a childhood dream
from its Disney sky

I would tell the voices to be quiet,
but then society would throw
me two cents under the rug
of alienation,

Not only two pennies
for my thoughts gone silent,

but two pennies with intrusive thoughts
who nightmare around street corners,

Afraid of being tossed back
into the wishing well of hospitals

where silence is the only answer
to not being punched and over medicated

I'd rather take those two pennies and
save them in a jar labeled SAFE

And hope with my holy accountant fingers
that one day my Cherry blossoms will bloom rainbows,

which speak to the sky in softer tones,
and do not scream, "Die" at me 12 times a day

Self-Medicate – 3

I pushed away the rain today,
and decided to drown
my spirit in fire instead

The liquid bruises
still ache, and
the belligerence
that is my waking skin
burned my mortality

I singed myself
at the altar of my hope
and poured the remnants
of my future into glass

All is black
All is black

Branches of the Same Tree

Some people think that depression
is just sadness and crying

The iceberg consumed with a hailstorm
upon its head known as depression
is only scratching its own surface

In fact, crying is the best you can possibly
hope for with depression

No one mentions the overwhelming pressure,
the numbness and the constant longing
to disappear from this flat thinking Earth

No one mentions the separation you feel
from yourself, completely isolated, feeling
like you're trapped within your own mind

No one mentions overwhelming thought
processes that you're never good enough,
or the Gordian's knot within your chest,
you sometimes wish to hang yourself with

In fact, No one mentions the panoramic
isolation that comes with just being depressed,
the Titans caught between two stones and
the two hard places which call themselves Stigma

To reach out and grab the vine of help
is for many, just too difficult to do

This catastrophic betrayal of the human
condition within the sphere of society
leads to the number one cause of death
for males under 50. Suicide

Now for a serious PSA: If you or anyone
you know is suffering from depression
Let them know you're there and that you care

Self-Medicate - 4

All Summer Long,
I've been dead to the mirror

Marker-black eyelids stare back
into the confusion of my mind

I would celebrate, but
my leafy arms feel nothing
but the soil, begging me
to return to it
with bouquets
of my bones

And my heart?

Are hearts supposed
to explode like pins

escaping the golden thread
in hopes of finding chemical fate?

My legs are still in the honeymoon
cycle, their infatuation crystallizing
light like prison chandeliers

My fingers dance across delusional
ballrooms, skipping
rope with my synapses

The Trauma of Spiritual Flesh

I spoke to my trauma;
>It cried for a mother who once
>sheltered him, now caught in dementia

I spoke to my trauma;
>It reeked of needles jabbed into
>my waist by disorderly orderlies
>of a behavioral health unit

I spoke to my trauma;
>it spoke of being arrested
>while manic, helpless, and
>then being knocked out
>like a home run trophy
>by police

I spoke to my trauma;
>It spoke of my first relationship,
>crushed to pieces by fate

I spoke to my trauma;
>It doused itself in marijuana high school,
>where welts to the head and arms
>among big sluggers and feeling
>completely alone in a world I could not escape

I spoke to my trauma;
>It spoke of cigarette burns
>and razor blades covering
>my bed at night, while sleeping
>on a pillow of frustration

I spoke to my trauma;
    It dug its grave into my chest
    and refuses to come back to life,
    no matter how many times I summon
    it with hands of peace

I spoke to my trauma;
    It revealed a boy, trapped
    within a void, screaming
    for sanity among the insane
    and broken

I spoke to my trauma;
    It was a home filled with love
    and sacrifice, broken by separation
    and alienation.

I spoke to my trauma;
    It was piles of garbage I refused
    to clean, as I buried myself
    with anger

I spoke to my trauma;
    It was the smile of my father,
    broken by delusion and schizophrenia

replaced with paranoia, as our conversations
    turned one sided, talking to himself more
    than anyone else

I spoke my trauma;
    it was a mother who flipped switches
    from love to cold blank stares within seconds,
    from being so overused by everyone,
    decided to take my ADHD medication

I spoke to my trauma;
    It spoke of a strong family
    carrying garbage bags to haul
    clothes in by foot while being called
    Bums

I spoke to my trauma;
    it mutated into paranoia,
    yelling matches for months
    and two near strangulations

*

I spoke to my trauma;
    It also spoke of hope, that one day
    I could find joy in simple things

I went where the hope lived;
    I found appreciation in music and poetry,
    but mostly video games to block
    out the negativity

I went where the hope lived;
    and I found that reading
    was a sanctuary unto itself

I went where the hope lived;
    I found nature and friendships
    hidden behind the stained veneer
    of trauma

I went where the hope lived;
    I saw a therapist for the first
    time at age 16 who was willing
    to talk

I went where the hope lived;
> music swung from the nucleus
> of my being and held me together

I went where the hope lived;
> and stopped hanging out
> with people who used

An outcast with abusive, "friends"
> I decided simply to be alone

I went where the hope lived;
> I left the alleyways of Springfield
> and stayed at home, dropping out
> of high school

I went where the hope lived;
> I found community at the local
> community college and met people
> who had never even heard
> the term shooting bows and arrows

I went where the hope lived;
> and found treatment
> for my mental illness
> which I inherited

I spoke to my trauma;
> I went where the hope lived;

> and now all I can say is:
> Your best day is still yet to come
> give yourself a chance to live it

Self-Medicate – 5

Sobriety

Our dreams are on tap,
no more running from ourselves
into that morose evening battle

We swallowed our last few
fractals of light, but our darkness
will hold our heads

We filled ourselves today,
instead of waiting for the burn
of the liquid Sun to carve our initials
into our stomachs

Our vice is running
away from our diligence,
and

the emptiness,
the emptiness,
the emptiness,

is being filled once again.

In This Society,

Lies are the currency on which we feed

If we do not carry our secrets,
does our blood still hold our pain?

There is a term in Western Medicine,
which is the term, "Disease"

Loosely defined as a particular habit or disposition
adversely affecting a person

    By those standards, I am full of diseases

        I sit on my knees all day and pray
for the meds to straddle my brain with comfort

        I scratch the insides of my arms
like Powerball tickets, hoping to win the jackpot of
    continued breathing

        I twiddle my thumbs nervously,
as anxious as high horses caught in the stable

What I am diagnosed as is not me,
        is not my enemy,
                is not my friend,
                        is not
    me

My diagnosis
is just another label in a book;
        understanding, yet clinical
and as unflinching as a dictator's face

Everyone has a disease, just as everyone
has a stone they must drag everywhere they go

    We are human sized Sisyphus' walking around,
    pulled by the weight of determination and love

        You wouldn't judge a person for a tooth ache
            Why would you judge me for speaking
about a delusion?

        The dual delusion being
    society's misinformed view of us,
and the very pervasive delusion

that there isn't any hope.

To the Reader

I can't write a sonnet,
but I can tell you how
dark the deep end
of a swimming pool is

after being bullied
for 4 days straight,
while hoping to see
your spirit leave your body

I can't write a villanelle,
but I can tell you
how broken a heart can
become when confronted
with possible tragedy
after tragedy

I can write a haiku,
but I would rather
show you how beautiful
Cherry blossom trees
can be after spending
3 weeks in a behavioral
health unit

I can weave a word or two,
but life is full of mystery,
and a word or two

can't compare
to the light
when it enters
your eyes
upon waking

colophon

Break, by Adam Levon Brown,
was set with SITKA and ZEN NEW fonts
by SpiNDec, Treasure Coast, Florida
The covers were designed
by Kris Haggblom, Port Saint Lucie, Florida

www.ingramcontent.com/pod-product-compliance
Lightning Source LLC
Chambersburg PA
CBHW020131130526
44591CB00032B/644